EDWIN MORGAN TWENTIES

SPACE AND SPACES

CELEBRATING EDWIN MORGAN'S CENTENARY

Love

Scotland

Menagerie

Take Heart

Space and Spaces

EDWIN MORGAN TWENTIES

SPACE AND SPACES

SELECTED POEMS

Introduced by
Ken MacLeod

Polygon

in association with
Carcanet

First published in Great Britain in 2020 by
Polygon, an imprint of Birlinn Ltd, in association with
Carcanet Press Ltd

Birlinn Ltd
West Newington House
10 Newington Road
Edinburgh EH9 1QS

9 8 7 6 5 4 3 2 1

www.polygonbooks.co.uk

ISBN 978 1 84697 546 2

British Library Cataloguing-in-Publication Data
A catalogue record for this book is available
from the British Library.

The publisher gratefully acknowledges investment from
Creative Scotland towards the publication of this book.

Typeset in Verdigris MVB by Polygon, Edinburgh
Printed and bound by Gutenberg, Malta

CONTENTS

INTRODUCTION

'Bold Braithwaite Morgan' – it sounds like a pirate, or a firm of solicitors. It's the subtitle of *Penguin Modern Poets 15*, which in 1969 introduced the work of Edwin Morgan (alongside Alan Bold and Edward Braithwaite) to a wider readership. That wider readership included me. A space-age schoolboy determined to become a scientist, I had two literary passions: science fiction and poetry.

Poetry was respectable. Science fiction was not. Encountering them in one place was a shock: of recognition, of delight, of vindication. 'Archives' and 'The Computer's First Christmas Card' hinted at a science-fictional sensibility. 'A View of Things' held out a secret handshake:

What I love about poetry is its ion engine

You had to have read science fiction to know about ion engines! Only then could you grasp the line's metaphor: a tiny continuous thrust that can't lift you off Earth but can shift your orbit and, by mere persistence, take you a long way – to anywhere, in time.

This suspicion was confirmed by 'In Sobieski's Shield' and 'From the Domain of Arnheim'. These poems were indeed science fiction, and not just any science fiction. Not your respectable science fiction, your Penguin Modern Classics *Nineteen Eighty-Four* or *Brave New World*, or even *The Day of the Triffids*, your science-fiction-for-people-who-don't-like-science-fiction. No, this was the pure quill, the hard stuff: pulp SF, Golden Age SF! The sort of science fiction you had to hide the covers of at home.

Many years later, on a visit to record Edwin Morgan's welcome to the 2005 World Science Fiction Convention in Glasgow, I asked him whether he read science fiction. Oh yes, he said, he found it stimulated the imagination. In his youth it had been frowned on, and he'd had to hide the covers of *Astounding* and *Amazing Stories* when he smuggled them into the house.

Other poets, of course, have written science fiction and space poetry. Few have taken it as seriously and unapologetically as Morgan, as an exercise of imagination valid on its own terms. Time travel, space travel, matter transmission across light-years, surviving the death of the Sun . . . all are taken literally, and their human consequences unravelled.

Morgan was likewise sure-footed with science fiction taken metaphorically. 'The First Men on Mercury' wouldn't work its spell for any other planet, and especially not for any planet ever taken seriously as a possible abode of life. 'The First Men on Mars'? 'The First Men on Venus'? *Aw, come on* . . . You see the problem. It's the impossibility (well, let's hedge our bets and say the extreme improbability) of intelligent, articulate life on Mercury that frees us to read the poem on its many other levels beyond our 'little plastic model / of the solar system, with working parts.'

Space, and spaces: the physical spaces on the page are indispensable to 'Spacepoem 3: Off Course', conveying the experience of microgravity with the same precision as it predicts the fate that Apollo 13 barely avoided. The use, as in this poem, of repetition and variation is a formal experiment Morgan often replicated. In 'Thoughts of a Module' the four-word phrases evoke the details of a moon landing, and the clipped laconic speech of astronauts, through the heroically compressed data processing of the onboard Apollo Guidance Computer, with its sixteen bits to a 'word'. In 'Instamatic the Moon February 1973' a spacecraft's subjectivity is more playfully explored, as the machine confronts an anomaly from the future: the 2001 that science fiction and film had already projected. And the deceptively 'mechanical' rearrangements – all meaningful – in 'Opening the Cage: 14 Variations on 14 Words' deliver a tolling rebuke to the glib nihilism of the original. The Earth beneath the stars, at its grimmest, resounds in the anguished, angered staccato of 'Starryveldt'.

'The Mouth' is a phantasmagoria, in explicit dialogue with the biblical apocalypse in which the heavens are rolled up like a scroll and the stars fall to Earth. The universe science has revealed simply swallows that older revelation's world, and world-view, whole. By contrast, 'A Vanguard' takes us to the brink of hell, an edge all the more terrifying on a spherical rather than a flat earth, leaving us to 'shiver at celestial mechanics / crumbling away.'

In the 1960s, space travel vaulted from fiction to fact: Gagarin to Apollo, always in the news. Since then we've seen robot probes, shuttle triumphs and disasters, images beamed back from Pluto of all amazing places, hundreds of men and women make the International Space Station their fleeting home in space. It has been an astounding human achievement. Yet for its sustained reflection in literature we must still turn to science fiction, and poetry – most notably the poetry of Edwin Morgan and poets influenced by him. Is this not strange? And shouldn't we change that?

> . . . it's hard
> to go let's go.

Ken MacLeod

SPACE AND SPACES

SPACEPOEM 3: OFF COURSE

the golden flood   the weightless seat
the cabin song   the pitch black
the growing beard   the floating crumb
the shining rendezvous   the orbit wisecrack
the hot spacesuit   the smuggled mouth-organ
the imaginary somersault   the visionary sunrise
the turning continents   the space debris
the golden lifeline   the space walk
the crawling deltas   the camera moon
the pitch velvet   the rough sleep
the crackling headphone   the space silence
the turning earth   the lifeline continents
the cabin sunrise   the hot flood
the shining spacesuit   the growing moon
   the crackling somersault   the smuggled orbit
   the rough moon   the visionary rendezvous
   the weightless headphone   the cabin debris
   the floating lifeline   the pitch sleep
   the crawling camera   the turning silence
   the space crumb   the crackling beard
   the orbit mouth-organ   the floating song

From Glasgow to Saturn
(Carcanet Press, 1973)

[3]

ARCHIVES

generation upon
generation upon
generation upon
generation upon
generation upon
generation upon
generation upon
generation upon
generation upon
generation upon
generation upon
generation upon
generation upon
generation upon
generation upon
generation upon
generation upon
generation upon
generation upon
g neration upon
g neration up n
g nerat on up n
g nerat n up n
g nerat n p n
g erat n p n

```
g   era   n  p  n
g   era   n     n
g   er    n     n
g    r    n     n
g         n     n
g         n
g
```

Gnomes

(Akros Publications, 1968)

THE COMPUTER'S FIRST
CHRISTMAS CARD

jolly merry
holly berry
jolly berry
merry holly
happy jolly
jolly jelly
jelly belly
belly merry
holly heppy
jolly Molly
marry Jerry
merry Harry
hoppy Barry
heppy Jarry
boppy heppy
berry jorry
jorry jolly
moppy jelly
Molly merry
Jerry jolly

```
b  e  l  l  y  b  o  p  p  y
j  o  r  r  y  h  o  p  p  y
h  o  l  l  y  m  o  p  p  y
B  a  r  r  y  m  e  r  r  y
J  a  r  r  y  h  a  p  p  y
h  a  p  p  y  b  o  p  p  y
b  o  p  p  y  j  o  l  l  y
j  o  l  l  y  m  e  r  r  y
m  e  r  r  y  m  e  r  r  y
m  e  r  r  y  m  e  r  r  y
m  e  r  r  y  C  h  r  i  s
a  m  m  e  r  r  y  a  s  a
C  h  r  i  s  m  e  r  r  y
a  s  M  E  R  R  Y  C  H  R
Y  S  A  N  T  H  E  M  U  M
```

Starryveldt

(Eugen Gomringer Press, 1965)

THE FIRST MEN ON MERCURY

– We come in peace from the third planet.
Would you take us to your leader?

– Bawr stretter! Bawr. Bawr. Stretterhawl?

– This is a little plastic model
of the solar system, with working parts.
You are here and we are there and we
are now here with you, is this clear?

– Gawl horrop. Bawr. Abawrhannahanna!

– Where we come from is blue and white
with brown, you see we call the brown
here 'land', the blue is 'sea', and the white
is 'clouds' over the land and sea, we live
on the surface of the brown land,
all round is sea and clouds. We are 'men'.
Men come –

– Glawp men! Gawrbenner menko. Menhawl?

– Men come in peace from the third planet
which we call 'earth'. We are earthmen.
Take us earthmen to your leader.

– Thmen? Thmen? Bawr. Bawrhossop.
Yuleeda tan hanna. Harrabost yuleeda.

– I am yuleeda. You see my hands,
we carry no benner, we come in peace.
The spaceways are all stretterhawn.

– Glawn peacemen all horrabhanna tantko!
Tan come at'mstrossop. Glawp yuleeda!

– Atoms are peacegawl in our harraban.
Menbat worrabost from tan hannahanna.

– You men we know bawrhossoptant. Bawr.
We know yuleeda. Go strawg backspetter quick.

– We cantantabawr, tantingko backspetter now!

– Banghapper now! Yes, third planet back
Yuleeda will go back blue, white, brown
nowhanna! There is no more talk.

– Gawl han fasthapper?

– No. You must go back to your planet.
Go back in peace, take what you have gained
but quickly.

 – Stretterworra gawl, gawl...

– Of course, but nothing is ever the same,
now is it? You'll remember Mercury.

From Glasgow to Saturn
(Carcanet Press, 1973)

FROM THE DOMAIN OF ARNHEIM

And so that all these ages, these years
we cast behind us, like the smoke-clouds
dragged back into vacancy when the rocket springs –

The domain of Arnheim was all snow, but we were there.
We saw a yellow light thrown on the icefield
from the huts by the pines, and laughter came up
floating from a white corrie
miles away, clearly.
We moved on down, arm in arm,
I know you would have thought it was a dream
but we were there. And those were trumpets –
tremendous round the rocks –
while they were burning fires of trash and mammoths' bones.
They sang naked, and kissed in the smoke.
A child, or one of their animals, was crying.
Young men blew the ice crystals off their drums.
We came down among them, but of course
they could see nothing, on their time-scale.
Yet they sensed us, stopped, looked up – even into our eyes.
To them we were a displacement of the air,
a sudden chill, yet we had no power
over their fear. If one of them had been dying

he would have died. The crying
came from one just born: that was the cause
of the song. We saw it now. What had we stopped
but joy?
I know you felt
the same dismay, you gripped my arm, they were waiting
for what they knew of us to pass.
A sweating trumpeter took
a brand from the fire with a shout and threw it
where our bodies would have been –
we felt nothing but his courage.
And so they would deal with every imagined power
seen or unseen.
There are no gods in the domain of Arnheim.

We signalled to the ship; got back;
our lives and days returned to us, but
haunted by deeper souvenirs than any rocks or seeds.
From time the souvenirs are deeds.

The Second Life
(Edinburgh University Press, 1968)

A HOME IN SPACE

Laid-back in orbit, they found their minds.
They found their minds were very clean and clear.
Clear crystals in swarms outside were their fireflies and larks.
Larks they were in lift-off, swallows in soaring.
Soaring metal is flight and nest together.
Together they must hatch.
Hatches let the welders out.
Out went the whitesuit riggers with frames as light as air.
Air was millions under lock and key.
Key-ins had computers wild on Saturday nights.
Nights, days, months, years they lived in space.
Space shone black in their eyes.
Eyes, hands, food-tubes, screens, lenses, keys were one.
One night – or day – or month – or year – they all –
all gathered at the panel and agreed –
agreed to cut communication with –
with the earth base – and it must be said they were –
were cool and clear as they dismantled the station and –
and gave their capsule such power that –
that they launched themselves outwards –
outwards in an impeccable trajectory, that band –
that band of tranquil defiers, not to plant any –

any home with roots but to keep a –
a voyaging generation voyaging, and as far –
as far as there would ever be a home in space –
space that needs time and time that needs life.

Star Gate: Science Fiction Poems

(Third Eye Centre, 1979)

IN SOBIESKI'S SHIELD

well the prophets were dancing in the end much
good it did them and the sun didn't rise at all
anywhere but we weren't among the frozen we had been
dematerialized the day before solar withdrawal
in a hurry it's true but by the best technique
who said only technique well anyhow the best
available and here we are now rematerialized
to the best of my knowledge on a minor planet
of a sun in Sobieski's Shield in our right mind I hope
approximately though not unshaken and admittedly
not precisely those who set out if one can
speak of it by that wellworn tellurian euphemism
in any case molecular reconstitution is no
sinecure even with mice and I wouldn't have been
utterly surprised if some of us had turned out
mice or worse

but at least not that or not yet the effects
of violent change are still slightly present an
indescribable stringent sensation like perhaps being
born or dying but no neither of these I am
very nearly who I was I see I have only
four fingers on my left hand and there's a sharp
twinge I never had in my knee and one most curious
I almost said birthmark and so it is in a sense

light brown shaped like a crazy heart spreading
across my right forearm well let it be we are
here my wife my son the rest of the laboratory
my wife has those streaks of fiery red in her
hair that is expected in women she looks very
frightened yet and lies rigid the rematerialization
is slow in her but that is probably better yes
her eyes flutter to mine questioning I nod can I
smile I think I can does she see me yes thank god
she is hardly altered apart from that extraordinarily
strange and beautiful crown of bright red hair
I draw her head into my arms and hide the sobbing
shuddering first breaths of her second life I don't
know what made me use that phrase who are we
if we are not who we were we have only
one life though we are huddled now in our
protective dome on this harsh metallic plain
that belches cobalt from its craters under a
white-bronze pulsing gong of a sun it was all
they could do for us light-years away it seemed suitable
dematerialization's impossible over short distances anyway
so let's start moving I can surely get onto my feet
yes hoy there

my son is staring fascinated at my four fingers
you've only one nipple I tell him and it's true
but for compensation when he speaks his boy's
treble has broken and at thirteen he is a man
what a limbo to lose childhood in where has
it gone between the throwing of a switch and these
alien iron hills across so many stars his blue eyes
are the same but there's a new graveness of the
second life that phrase again we go up together
to the concave of the dome the environment after all
has to be studied

is that a lake of mercury I can't quite see
through the smoke of the fumarole it's lifting now
but there's something puzzling even when I
my memory of mercury seems to be confused with
what is it blood no no mercury's not like blood
what then what is it I'm remembering or nearly
remembering look dad mercury he says and so it
must be but I see a shell-hole filled with rain-water
red in the sinking sun I know that landscape too

one of the wars far back twentieth century I think the
great war was it called France Flanders fields I remember
reading these craters waterlogged with rain mud blood
I can see a stark hand brandishing nothing through placid scum
in a lull of the guns what horror that the livid water
is not shaken by the pity of the tattoo on the dead arm
a heart still held above the despair of the mud
my god the heart on my arm my second birth mark
the rematerialization has picked up these fragments I have
a graft of war and ancient agony forgive
me my dead helper

the sulky pool of mercury stares back at me I am
seeing normally now but I know these flashes will return
from the far past times I gather my wife and son to me
with a fierce gesture that surprises them I am not
a demonstrative man yet how to tell them
what and who I am that we are bound to all that lived
though the barriers are unspeakable we know a little of that
but something what is it gets through it is not
an essence but an energy how it pierces how it

clutches for still as I run my hand through her
amazing hair streaming on my shoulder I feel
a fist shaken in a shell-hole turn in my very marrow
we shall live in the rings of this chain the jeremiahs
who said nothing human would stand are confounded if I cry
even the dry tear in my heart that I cannot
stop or if I laugh to think they thought they
could divide the indivisible the old moon's in
the new moon's arms let's take our second
like our first life out from the dome are the suits
ready the mineral storm is quieter it's hard
to go let's go

The Second Life
(Edinburgh University Press, 1968)

INSTAMATIC THE MOON
FEBRUARY 1973

At the edge of the Sea of Serenity,
where the grey dust rises into foothills
of the Taurus Mountains, a confrontation
takes place. An unmanned, eight-wheeled steam pram,
Lunokhod-2, sophisticatedly clumsy as an
Emmet velocipede, has stopped its trundle
faced by a large, hard, blank, slab-like stone.
Busily it winks, and scans the monolith,
registering back to Tass
an impossible smoothness.
What crater could eject this unpitted stele
that stands marking nothing?
Too much simplicity is a headache for lunokhods,
and the moonrover has focused, in its frenzy for data,
on a spider-web of shadows and scratches at the base of the slab
which imagination might just read in Ventris mood
as K space BRI query space K query.

Star Gate: Science Fiction Poems
(Third Eye Centre, 1979)

[20]

THE MOUTH

I saw a great mouth in space that fifty thousand angels
    could not fill
they ran shrieking from it as it grew and threw their
    coloured coats and flares
for lures among the stars while it advanced and swallowed
    the planets of the sun
one by one and then the sun

it rose and swayed the Milky Way collapsed into it like a
    poorly shuffled pack
deeper and deeper into darkness it brought darkness and
    what it blotted out
it grew drunk on to grinning-point with so much fire in its
    belly it roared
over its thankless hoard

for that was the new horror to hear it when it howled like a
    hungry scraped womb
and galaxies jampacked with glittering rayed-out million-
    year-old civilizations
were jumped like a handful of asteroids and sucked into
    tales of hell
for all they could tell

the Plough long gone the winding Dragon the Lyre the
    Balance the fading Charioteer
Aquarius with a loud cry Keel Stern and Sails in terrible
    rushing silence
and now white Sirius was black yellow Capella was black
    red Antares was black
and no lights ever came back

heavens and paradises popped like seaweed eternal laws
    were never seen again
angels' teeth were cosmic dust and cosmic dust was angels'
    teeth all's grist
to that dark mill where christs and godbearers were pulped
    with their domes ikons vanes
their scrolls aeons and reigns

in Virgo the most evolved life there was was calm and
    watchful in its fiery coverts
the mouth had long been computed probable and plans had
    been laid and re-laid
the dense cluster of three thousand galaxies had made itself
    a force field
that would not know how to yield

the worlds of Virgo were not only inhabited but
    hyperinhabited they were all
one life and their force field was themselves they were a wall
    they shone they stood
jehovahs and elohim are daguerreotypes to their movies
    they made universes
as poets make verses

in Virgo they did not underestimate the mouth they were
    the last star-gate and goal
when they saw there were no other lights in the recesses of
    space and it was hard
to distinguish the shadow of the unsated mouth from the
    shadow of the dead
but its lips were blackest red

they gaped for Virgo with a scream they gaped for Virgo with a
scream they gaped for Virgo with a scream they gaped for Virgo
with a scream they gaped for Virgo with a scream they gaped
at that great quiet gate

Star Gate: Science Fiction Poems
(Third Eye Centre, 1979)

O PIONEERS!

THIS TUNNEL WAS BUGN BEGUBNUGN IN 1880

WILLIAM SHARP

Workman's inscription on entrance to abandoned
Channel Tunnel at Dover

Channel Tunnel bugn.
1880. Sharp Wilgn.

Tannel Chunnel begum.
8018. Shart Willum.

Tennal Chennul gbung.
8081. Shant Willung.

Chennul Tennal bengug.
8108. Shunt Willibug.

Chunnal Tennel begbugn.
8801. Slunt Willubugmn.

Chuntenlannel begubnugn.

8810. Blunt Wuglbumlugn.

****

10880. Brigde bugn.

Starryveldt
(Eugen Gomringer Press, 1965)

OPENING THE CAGE:
14 VARIATIONS ON 14 WORDS

I have nothing to say and I am saying it and that is poetry.
                                              John Cage

I have to say poetry and is that nothing and am I saying it
I am and I have poetry to say and is that nothing saying it
I am nothing and I have poetry to say and that is saying it
I that am saying poetry have nothing and it is I and to say
And I say that I am to have poetry and saying it is nothing
I am poetry and nothing and saying it is to say that I have
To have nothing is poetry and I am saying that and I say it
Poetry is saying I have nothing and I am to say that and it
Saying nothing I am poetry and I have to say that and it is
It is and I am and I have poetry saying say that to nothing
It is saying poetry to nothing and I say I have and am that
Poetry is saying I have it and I am nothing and to say that
And that nothing is poetry I am saying and I have to say it
Saying poetry is nothing and to that I say I am and have it

The Second Life

(Edinburgh University Press, 1968)

PARTICLE POEMS

1.
The old old old old particle
smiled. 'I grant you I'm not beautiful,'
he said, 'but I've got charm.
It's charm that's led me where I am.'

Opened up his bosom, showed me a quark.
It gleamed. He grinned like a clam. 'Sort
of heart, really, though I've got four.
They're in orbit, and what for

is a good question, unless to pump up
charm. I know I must look a frump
– just fishing – but seriously
would you not say I'm easily

the nearest thing to doom and centrehood
you've ever been unable to preclude?
Cathedrals – oh, antiquities and slime,
knucklebones, teeth five feet long, signs

and wonders, auks, knuckledusters,
twangs from armchairs, waters
waiting to break, cells waiting to squeak,
a sniff of freesia, a book

of hours, and hours themselves like days
in love, and even nanoseconds raised
by charm to higher powers, wait
until I make them, and fade.'

Shot off – never showed his age.

II.
The young particle screamed round the bend,
braked hard, broke.
His mother dozing in Manchuria
heard his last cry. A mare's ear twitched.
Dust, and dust, the wires sang.

III.
Three particles lived in mystical union.
They made knife, fork, and spoon,
and earth, sea, and sky.
They made animal, vegetable, and mineral,
and faith, hope, and charity.
They made stop, caution, go,
and hickory, dickory, dock.

They made yolk, white, and shell,
and hook, line, and sinker.
They made pounds, shillings, and pence,
and Goneril, Regan, and Cordelia.
They made Shadrach, Meshach, and Abednego,
and game, set, and match.

A wandering particle kidnapped one of them,
and the two that were left made day and night,
and left and right, and right and wrong,
and black and white, and off and on,
but things were never quite the same,
and two will always yearn for three.
They're after you, or me.

IV.
Part particle and part idea, she
struggled through a throb of something.
A wheatear, or an ear of wheat?
How could she possibly know
beyond the shrill vibrations, sunny fibres, field?
What was the field but forces, surges?
To veins of green and veins of red

she was colour-blind. Well, she was blind.
But was she there at all –
when the wind ruffled that nest of growing things
and it took its course in the sun?

v.
The particle that decided
got off its mark, but died.

vi.
Their mausoleum
is a frozen silent flak.
The fractured tracks,
photographed, docket
dead dogfights,
bursts of no malice.
Almost pure direction
points its stream,
deflected, detected.
Better than ogam
or cuneiform the tracer
of telling particles

fans out angrily
itself, itself, itself –
who we were
were here, here,
we died at the crossroads
or we defected
or we raced ahead
to be burnt out.
Faint paths hardly score,
yet shake the lens, end
in lucider mosaics
of theory. Go,
bid the soldiers shoot.

Star Gate: Science Fiction Poems
(Third Eye Centre, 1979)

STARRYVELDT

starryveldt
  slave
southvenus
  serve
SHARPEVILLE
  shove
shriekvolley
  swerve
shootvillage
  save
spoorvengeance
  stave
spadevoice
  starve
strikevault
  strive
subvert
  starve
smashverwoerd
  strive
scattervoortrekker
  starve
spadevow
  strive
sunvast

starve

survive

strive

SO: VAEVICTIS

Starryveldt

(Eugen Gomringer Press, 1965)

THOUGHTS OF A MODULE

It is black so. There is that dust.
My ladder in light. What are my men.
One is foot down. That is pack drill.
Black what is visor. A hiss I heard.
The talks go up. Clump now but float.
Is a jump nearer. A camera paced out.
I phase another man. Another man is second.
Second last feet on. The dust I think.
So some soles cross. Is a flag near.
No move yon flag. Which voice comes down.
White house thanks all. Command module man not.
Is kangaroo hop around. I think moon dance.
Or white bird is. Good oxygen I heard.
Earth monitors must be. Is it too pressing.
Trained man is gay. Fail safe is gay.
The black I see. What instruments are lonely.
Sharp is a shadow. A horizon goes flat.
All rock are samples. Dust taken I think.
Is bright my leg. In what sun yonder.
An end I think. How my men go.
The talks come down. The ladder I shake.

To leave that bright. Space dark I see.
Is my men last. Men are that first.
That moon is here. They have some dust.
Is home they know. Blue earth I think.
I lift I see. It is that command.
My men go back. I leave that here.
It is bright so.

From Glasgow to Saturn
(Carcanet Press, 1973)

A VANGUARD

We came to the end of the world at midnight.
Someone called out from the back of the column,
Is that it then? What is it like? I answered,
Whatever you have of imagination
you must use. Come forward. All of you. Stand easy.
Through so much dust, we were no smart company,
but somehow the tired group seemed monumental
as any old stone circle where they clustered
gravely over staves and rifles and brooded
above the yelling abyss we'd reached the lip of.
And those who thought a globe could never have one –
abyss, I mean, edge, rim, sick slope to vacancy –
began to shiver at celestial mechanics
crumbling away. It must be a ravine then,
fog, darkness, the farther bank is hidden –
one of them said, using imagination.
No one believed that rational man; the spirit
of the place, our chilling sweat, the terrible groaning
from throats unseen below our feet, took toll of
any reason we had left. What had we looked for
in fact but the end of the world, we the vanguard
sent out to scotch or seal appalling rumours.
So there we were. Was it hell? We saw no one.
The cold grew more intense. Let's go back then,
I said, it's not the end of the world. Joking

broke the spell. Someone laughed. A ravine surely,
windy caves and flues like voices. And supper
a short march away. Soon they would start whistling.
I kept my thoughts, but nothing would do, nothing.
No end in time was near, or in space possible.
As for the dead, who am I to appease them,
a scout, a ragged man, a storyteller?

Hold Hands among the Atoms
(Mariscat Press, 1991)

ABOUT THE AUTHOR

EDWIN MORGAN (1920–2010) was born in Glasgow, and spent his life there except for his six years with the Royal Army Medical Corps in the Middle East. He studied English Literature at the University of Glasgow, where he went on to teach, retiring as Professor Emeritus in 1980. He was appointed Glasgow's Poet Laureate in 1999, and awarded the Queen's Gold Medal for Poetry in 2000. In 2004 he was appointed the first Scots Makar of modern times, and wrote the poem 'For the Opening of the Scottish Parliament' in the same year. His poetry is praised for its linguistic inventiveness, social realism and humane curiosity. He wrote concrete and visual poetry, opera libretti and collaborated with jazz saxophonist Tommy Smith to set his work to music; he was also a translator, playwright and critic. Morgan's work is renowned for its outward-looking internationalism, his poetic gaze moving from Europe to the wider world and into space, yet always returning to Glasgow, whose people and landscape he so memorably evoked and imagined.